IT'S FUN TO LEARN ABOUT
WORDS

Claire Llewellyn
Consultant: Dr Naima Browne

ARMADILLO

NOTES

This book is packed full of busy scenes and words that will help your children to build up their vocabulary. Funny pictures and exciting activities encourage them to practise all the early reading and writing skills they need for their first years at school.

Learning with pictures

Stimulating pictures offer plenty of learning opportunities. Some of the pictures show everyday objects that your child will readily recognize. Others encourage your child to enter the world of the imagination, to tell stories and enjoy fantasy.

Reading together

Children like sharing books. You can help your child by reading aloud the words that accompany the pictures. You'll soon be doing it together! Point to the labels as you say each word. This will help your child to learn new words and develop early reading skills. Do not expect a child to read the book from cover to cover. Go through the book at your child's pace. Try to make reading times enjoyable.

Talking it through

Help your child's understanding by talking about the pictures. Help to relate them to your child's experience by talking about the things he or she does. Talking about the things that children know helps to develop self-confidence and the skills of listening and speaking.

Learning by doing

Encourage your child to try the activities. They have been specially designed to be easy and fun to do, and little preparation is required. They will extend your child's vocabulary and help them to develop their reading and writing skills.

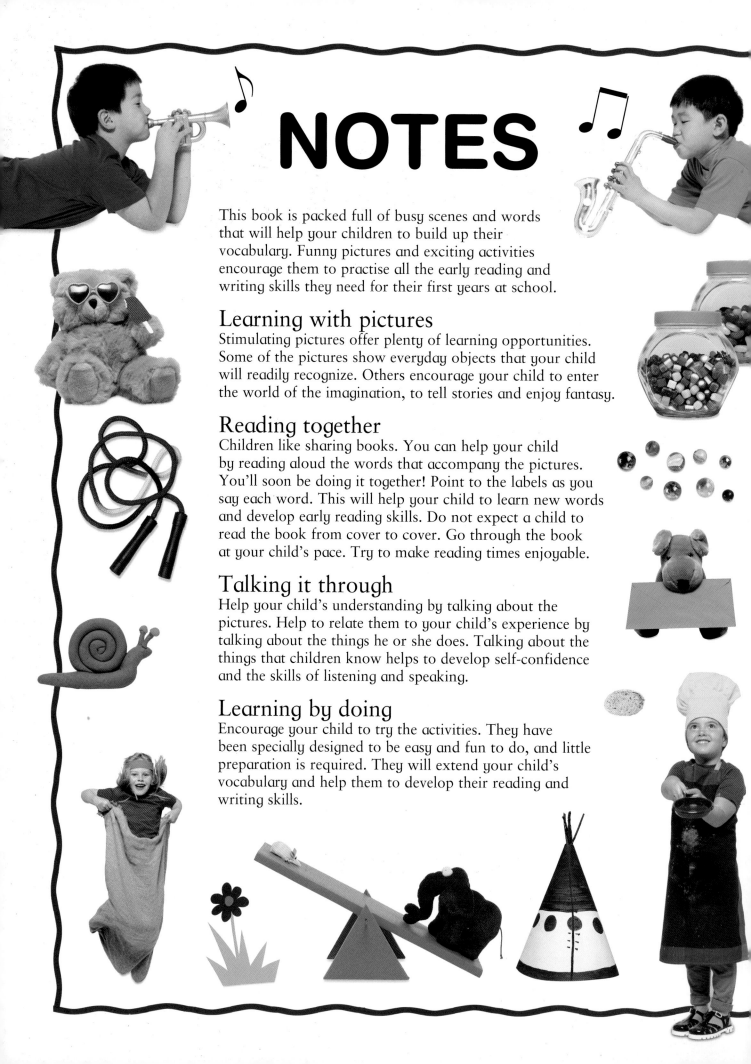

CONTENTS

4   Getting up, getting ready

6   Playgroup

8   Shopping

10   Cooks at work

12   Playtime

14   A good story

16   Moving along

18   Jobs for fun

20   Making music

22   Party time

24   Sunny seaside

26   Sport crazy

28   Action

30   Guessing game

Getting up, getting ready

Waking up

curtains

window

music player

boy

pillow

table

bedding

chest of drawers

dog basket

slippers

Getting dressed

baby suit

cardigan

shirt

jester's hat

t-shirt

socks

dress

jumpsuit

bootees

jeans

shoes

alarm clock

lamp

hairbrush

slippers

clothes hanger

sponge

rubb duc

In the bathroom

toothpaste

mirror

shelf

ing
d

bathtub

wind-up
toy

sponge

Hair fun

ribbon

hair gel

headband

scrunchies

Ready to go

rain hat

umbrella

raincoat

toy dog

rubber
boots

summer
dress

sun
hat

sandals

knitted
hat

coat

snow

soap

toothbrush

comb

scarf

gloves

5

Playgroup

Puppet show

stage

popcorn

audience

cushion

Water playtime

shells

play pots

watering can

Drawing

backpack

pencils

pencil pot

paper

felt-tipped pens

Snack time

bookshelves

books

cookies

milk

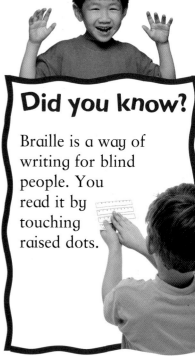

Did you know?

Braille is a way of writing for blind people. You read it by touching raised dots.

puppet

pencil

adhesive tape

pencil sharpener

eraser

tug boat

Cleaning up

duster

...ning ...ard

laundry

washing basket

dustpan

cuddly toys

Try this!

Make a poster

1. Cut out a square of bright paper. Stick a white label on it.

2. Write on it the name of your playgroup. Draw some of the friends you see there.

Fun Group

Painting

easel

apron

paint pots

green paint

Cutting and pasting

glitter

glue stick

picture

paper shapes

scissors

dustpan

brush

triangle

square

circle

blue paint

7

Shopping

Writing a shopping list

jar

shopping list

shopping basket

Try this!

Write a shopping list

Do you need anything from the supermarket? Write a list of the food you want to buy. Draw the food next to the word.

bread
ketchup
apples
soup
grapes

At the supermarket

washing powder

canned vegetables

fruit juice

cereal

shopping trolley

bread

bread basket

glass jars

jelly beans

candies

bananas

chocolates

strawberry

paper bag

till

8

uying fruit nd vegetables

Bananas

tomato

juggling Ted

pears

apples

bananas

sign

Apples

onions

cauliflowers

potatoes

Paying at the till

store assistant

customer

receipt

Supermarket

box

paper bag

plum

shopping basket

toilet roll

carrot

shopping trolley

purse

9

Cooks at work

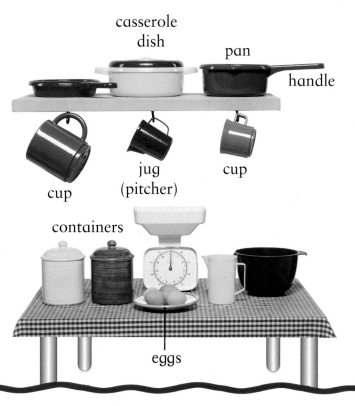

casserole dish

pan

handle

cup

jug (pitcher)

cup

containers

eggs

chef's hat

apron

oven

cookbooks

dial

stove

time

oven door

cooker

Try this!

Cake icing (frosting)

1. Pour 115g/4oz/1 cup of icing (confectioners') sugar into a bowl.

2. Add 120ml/4fl oz/ ½ cup of water to the sugar. Stir them together.

3. Mix in 5ml/1 tsp of red food dye. Now spread the mixture on to some cakes.

Decorating cupcakes

food dye

paper cases

cake decorations

piping bag

cupcakes

mixing bowl

whisk

frying pan

wooden spoons

casserole dish

Making pancakes

pancake

chocolate syrup

cream

honey

chef

table leg

Table setting

tablecloth

plate

bread plate

Washing dishes

dishwashing liquid

scourers

duster

gloves

bowl

Cleaning up

rubbish/ garbage container

cleaner

broom

soap suds

bucket

mop

napkin

scales

fork

knife

lemon

plate

spoon

brush

11

Playtime
Toy farm

cow

milk churns

chickens

fence

sheep

hay

fence post

farmer

pig

tractor

Trucks

crane

refuse/garbage truck

blocks

Try this!
Play 'I Spy'
Choose an object you can see in the room. Tell your friends which letter the word begins with. Can they guess what it is? Whoever guesses correctly is the next to choose.

dump truck

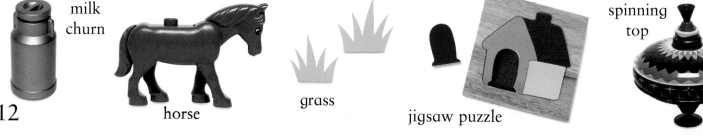

milk churn

horse

grass

jigsaw puzzle

spinning top

Outside

toy mouse

toy elephant

seesaw

tunnel

slide

steps

rocker

hopper

pond

Toys

toy bag

marbles

ng car

ll

Train set

signal

station master

station

funnel

carriage

steam train

train track

cement mixer

ball

flower

Jack-in-the-box

13

A good story

Fairy

wings

magic
wand

stars

mice

pumpkin

Witch

cobweb

broomstick

spide

potion
bottles

slime

snail

snail trail

King

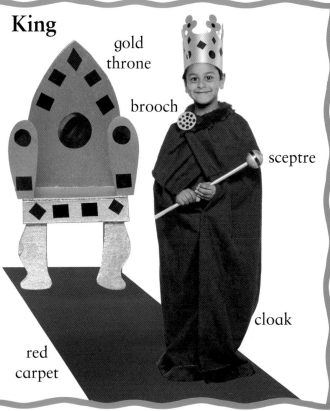

gold
throne

brooch

sceptre

cloak

red
carpet

Cowboy

saddle

belt

rocking horse

lasso

tassel

cowboy
boots

magic
wand

crown

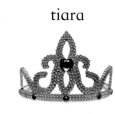

tiara

sceptre

cauldron

ates

parrot

pirate hat

treasure chest

map

spyglass

North American Indians

sticks

tepee

feather

flames

camp fire

Try this!

Write a potion recipe

1. What would you put in a potion? Think up a gruesome recipe. Then find a large piece of paper.

slime

bat juice

spider

mouse

2. Draw pictures of your gruesome ingredients. Write the name of each one beside it.

cowboy hat

gold necklace

spyglass

eye patch

earring

feather headdress

15

Moving along

Driving to the petrol (gas) station

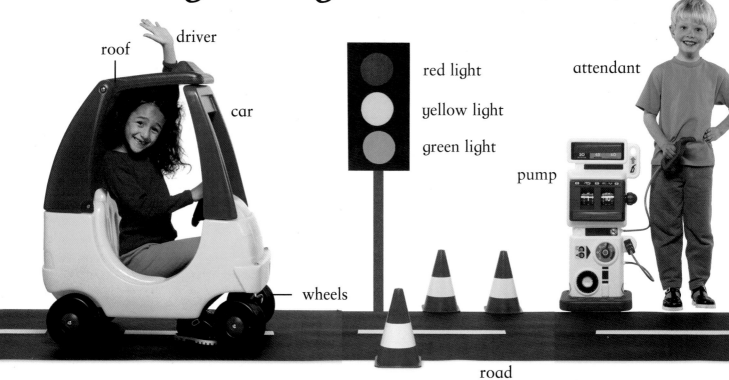

roof

driver

car

wheels

red light

yellow light

green light

attendant

pump

road

Cycling

bicycle

stabilizer

brake

handlebars

tricycle

seat

pedal

spokes

Skateboarding

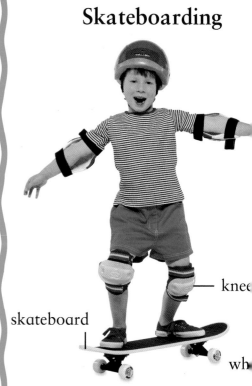

skateboard

knee

wh

steering
wheel

traffic
cone

elbow pads

helmet

traffic l

16

Flying

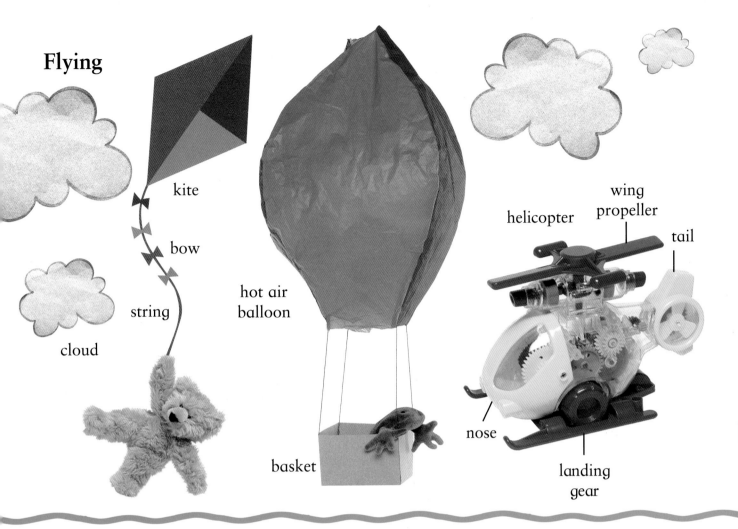

kite

bow

string

cloud

hot air balloon

basket

helicopter

wing propeller

tail

nose

landing gear

iling

sail

or

Try this!

Bus trip

1. Draw a picture of a bus that you would like to travel on. Invite some friends to join you.

2. Draw your friends in their seats. Then, write their names above them.

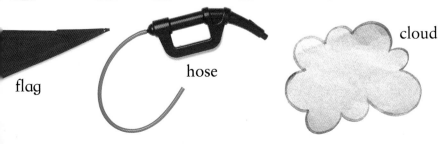

flag

hose

cloud

boat

safety ring

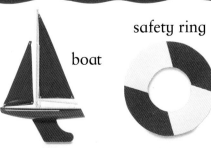

Jobs for fun

Doctor

stethoscope

lab coat

patient

first aid kit

Clown

wig

pom-pom

water squirter

Movie star

headband

feather boa

bracelet

dress

flowers

microphone

reporter

notepad

Carpenter

hard hat

tool shelf

spanner (wrench)

pliers

overalls

photographer

tool box

thermometer

bandage

bolts

telephone

plasters (Band-Aids)

Office worker

glasses

et

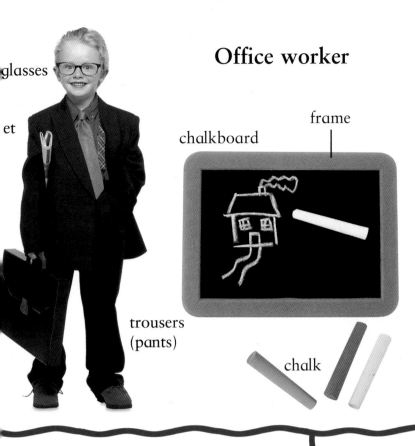

trousers
(pants)

chalkboard

frame

chalk

Try this!

Dream job

I'm a clown!
I work in a circus.

Think of the job
you'd most
like to do. Draw a
picture of the outfit
you would wear
for your job.
Draw a speech
bubble and then write
in it who you are.

Detective

Wanted

wanted
poster

hat magnifying
glass

pawprint

office
desk

nose

Astronaut

space helmet

space suit

spaceship

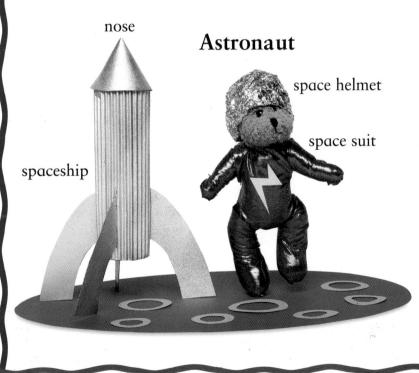

horn

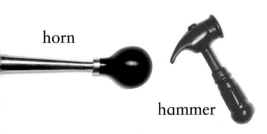

hammer

briefcase

tie

camera

Making music

Jazz band

mouthpiece

saxophone

bugle

trumpet

Ted rock band

drum

drummer

notes

Percussion music

castanets

guitarist

guitar

lead singer

Choir

ruffle collar

song sheet

singer

Did you know?

Music is written in notes, not words. The names of the notes are A, B, C, D, E, F and G.

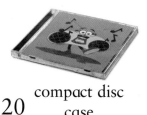

compact disc case

headphones

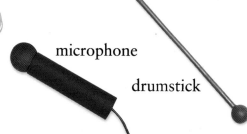

microphone

drumstick

sheet music

bato

ula dancer

maraca

grass skirt

ankle garland

Listening to music

headphones

radio

music player

compact discs

Orchestra

musicians

conductor

harmonica

baton

triangle

tcher

xylophone

maraca

loudspeaker

neck garland

tambourine

21

Party time

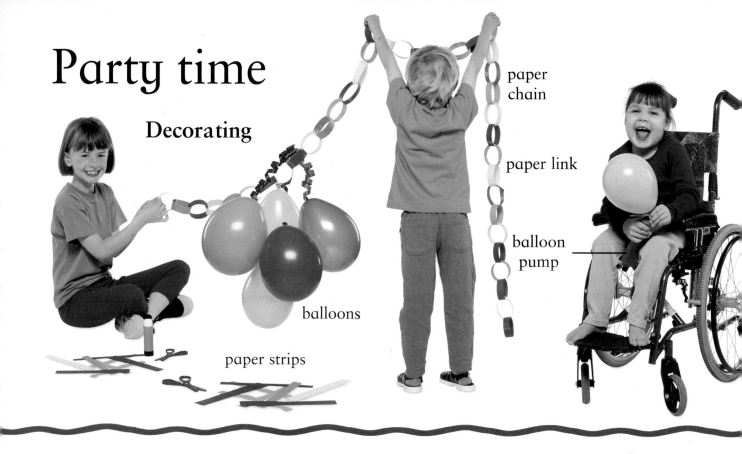

Decorating

paper chain

paper link

balloon pump

balloons

paper strips

Piles of presents

Happy Birthday

banner

birthday girl

presents

party guest

Try this!

Decorate a cake

1. Buy or make a cake. Write your age on the top.

2. Sprinkle on decorations. Add the right number of candles.

birthday card

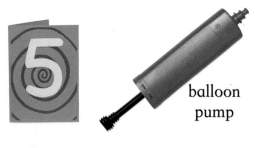
balloon pump

bow

tarts

party hat

Party treats

crisps (chips)

drinking straw

pizza

cookies

sandwiches

Magic show

audience

plate spinner

acrobat

magician

cape

trick box

magic wand

birthday cake

top hat

ribbon

candle

Sunny seaside

At the beach

sun

sun umbrella

sunbather

surfboard

beach bag

towel

Fishing

baseball cap

fishing net

Did you know?

Sometimes symbols are used instead of words.

This sign means that there is water ahead.

This sign means that children cross here.

shells

pincers

rock pool

sand

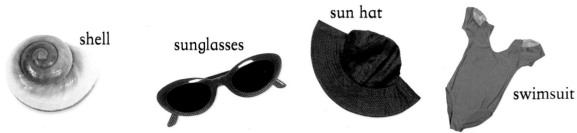

shell

sunglasses

sun hat

swimsuit

cr

Ready for a swim

snorkel

armband

swimmer

swimming hat

inflatable raft

sponge

starfish

freshments

Ice Cream

ice cream sign

ice lolly (popsicle)

ice cream

sandcastle

sand shapes

Playing

sun hat

beach ball

bucket

sandals

spade (shovel)

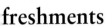

ice cube tray

flippers

goggles

ring

sunscreen

Sport crazy

Soccer

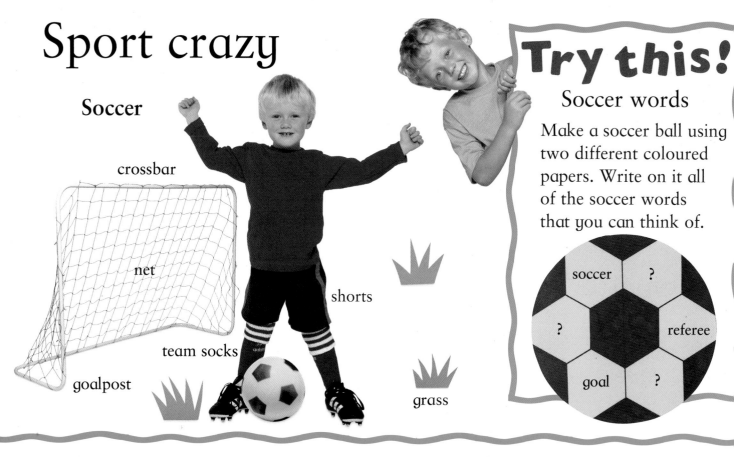

crossbar

net

goalpost

team socks

shorts

grass

Try this!

Soccer words

Make a soccer ball using two different coloured papers. Write on it all of the soccer words that you can think of.

soccer

?

?

referee

goal

?

Sports day

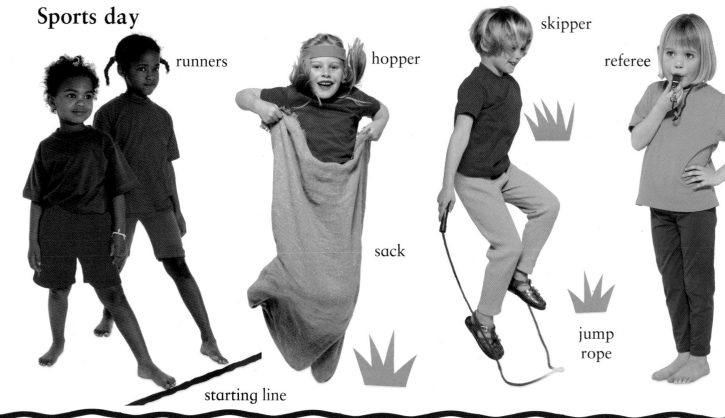

runners

hopper

skipper

referee

sack

jump rope

starting line

soccer ball

soccer boots

golf tee

whistle

golf ball

26

Golf

caddie

golf hole

leisure shoes

Basketball

hoop

sweat suit top

basketball net

sweat suit bottoms

sneakers

Activities

tennis racket

weight lifter

tennis skirt

headband

weight

tennis player

Gymnastics

feet

legs

leotard

handstand

wristband

mat

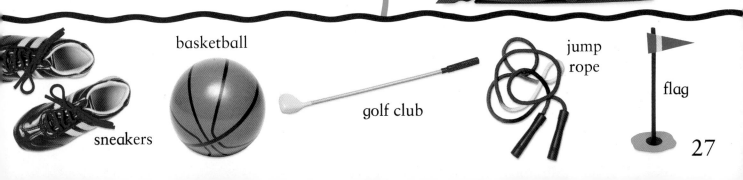

basketball

sneakers

golf club

jump rope

flag

Action

smiling

kissing

hugg[ing]

hopping

sitting

eating

crossing legs

floating

blowing

pulling

licking

sitting

dangling

giggling

clapping

kneeling

standing

sitting

splashing

laughing

bending

Try this!

Fun action game

Think of a fun action word. Tell your friend
what it is. Now, ask them to act it out.
Take it in turns to play. You could . . .

. . . wriggle like a snake.

. . . or hop like a frog.

Guessing game

Think of the word for one of the pictures on these pages. When you've thought of it, find the word and cover it with a button or marker. Look for another word. Continue until you've covered all the circles.

You will need 34 buttons or markers

tiara

fork

hairbrush

balloons

horn

plate

snail

cowboy hat

camera

chef

sunglasses

traffic cone

racing car

microphone

paint

flippers

whistle

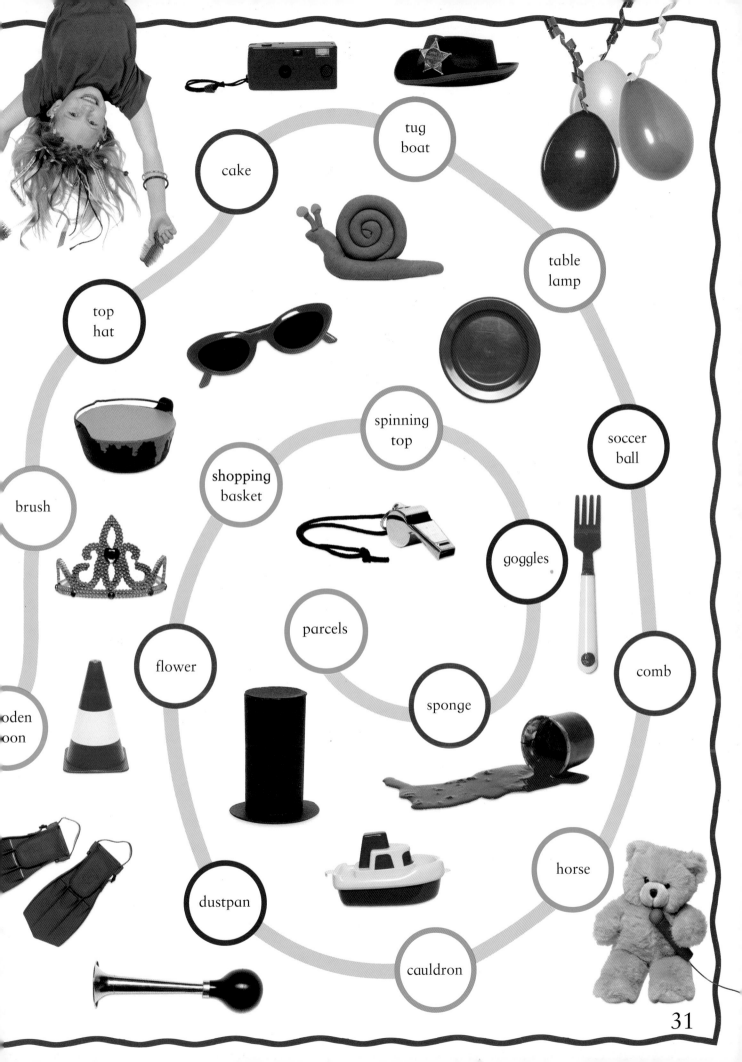

tug
boat

cake

table
lamp

top
hat

soccer
ball

spinning
top

shopping
basket

brush

goggles

parcels

comb

flower

sponge

oden
oon

horse

dustpan

cauldron

This edition is published by Armadillo,
an imprint of Anness Publishing Ltd,
108 Great Russell Street,
London WC1B 3NA;
info@anness.com

www.annesspublishing.com; twitter: @Anness_Books

Anness Publishing has a new picture agency outlet
for images for publishing, promotions or advertising.
Please visit our website www.practicalpictures.com
for more information.

A CIP catalogue record for this book
is available from the British Library.

Publisher: Joanna Lorenz
Senior Editor: Felicity Forster
Educational Consultant: Dr Naima Browne,
    Department of Education, University of London
Photography: John Freeman
Stylist: Melanie Williams
Designer: Mike Leaman Design Partners
Production Controller: Ben Worley

PUBLISHER'S NOTE

Manufacturer: Anness Publishing Ltd,
108 Great Russell Street, London WC1B 3NA, England
For Product Tracking go to: www.annesspublishing.com/tracking
Batch: 7556-23902-1127

ACKNOWLEDGEMENTS
The publisher would like to thank the following children for
appearing in this book: Africa, Alice, Andrew, April, Daisy, Faye,
Grace, Harriet, Holly, Jackson, James, Jasmine, Jonathan, Joseph,
Kadeem, Lucie, Luke, Madison, Milo, Miriam, Otis, Philip, Rebeka
Rhys, Safari, Samantha, Sumaya, Tom, Zaafir, Zamour.

d e k

n g t

y m